THE
Archive Photographs
SERIES

IRLAM AND CADISHEAD

Arms of Irlam Urban District Council. These were presented on the occasion of the Diamond Jubilee of the council in 1955 by Sir John James. The shield is from the Manor of Barton, the lion from the De Hultons and the flail from the De Traffords. The blue indented chief is that of the Lathoms, the principal family of Irlam in the sixteenth, seventeenth and eighteenth centuries. The boars' heads are from the arms of the Booths of Barton who held Irlam and Cadishead from the thirteenth century. The mitre is from Stanlaw Abbey, which held Cadishead from the thirteenth century to the Dissolution. The crest symbolises more recent history: the steel rim with flames represents the steel industry. The eagle is the crest of the nineteenth century Greaves family; the 'fountain' on its breast is for the rivers Mersey and Irwell and the Ship Canal. The motto means 'by skill and wisdom'.

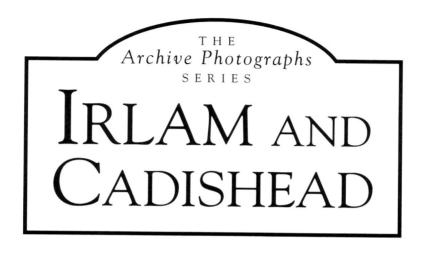

THE
Archive Photographs
SERIES

IRLAM AND CADISHEAD

Compiled by
Marion Beeston and Irlam and Cadishead Local History Society

CHALFORD

First published 1997
Copyright © Marion Beeston and
Irlam and Cadishead Local History Society, 1997

The Chalford Publishing Company
St Mary's Mill, Chalford,
Stroud, Gloucestershire, GL6 8NX

ISBN 0 7524 0712 0

Typesetting and origination by
The Chalford Publishing Company
Printed in Great Britain by
Bailey Print, Dursley, Gloucestershire

A popular postcard of many years ago showing the Manchester Ship Canal, Old River and the Boat House, the Boat House Inn, the New Soap Works, Irlam Parish Church and the main road near the Moorfield Parade.

Contents

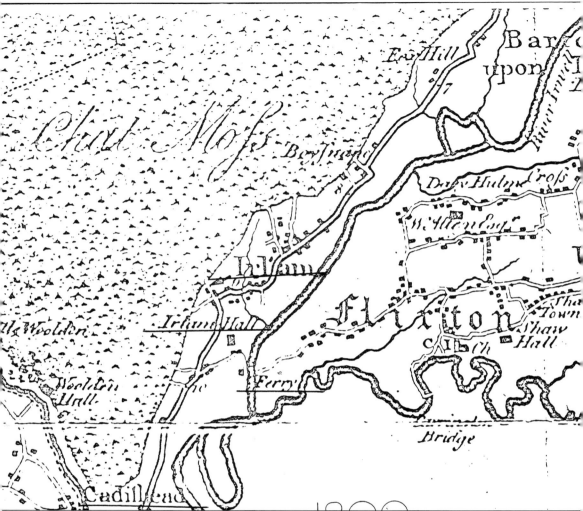

This map of 1800 illustrates the isolated position of Irlam and Cadishead, with Chat Moss on one side and the Rivers Irwell and Mersey on the other, leaving a narrow corridor of land between.

Introduction

The early growth of Irlam and Cadishead, known in earlier days as Irwelham and Cadwallishead, was somewhat restricted by the fact that the Rivers Irwell and Mersey ran along one side of the area and the great Chat Moss on the other. The rivers and the Moss left a narrow corridor of land between of varying widths, from about a half mile to a mile; this is known nowadays as a ribbon development. The main highway from Manchester to Liverpool, via Warrington, ran through this corridor and from early days was recognised as the King's Highway.

Some form of agriculture was practised locally and more so after the land in Cadishead was granted to the Abbot of Stanlow, Irlam being granted to the Cannons of Cockersand. Regular visits would have been made in order to minister to the people's religious needs and also to collect rents and other dues. These regular travellers would call at some of the farm houses for rest and refreshment. The farmers, who brewed their own beer, would have taken out a licence and thus their farms became inns supplying both the travellers and the local people, who were dependent upon agriculture and weaving for their living.

Most goods were transported by pack horse and with the steady increase in trade between Manchester and Liverpool, the roads deteriorated and became costly to maintain. This led to a survey of the Rivers Irwell and Mersey in 1712 with the idea of reducing the ever increasing cost of transport by using packet boats. By 1725 goods were being transported by barges. Wharves were built at a Higher and Lower Irlam and at Cadishead, on both sides of the rivers, making the villages more important and thus increasing their population.

In 1753 turnpiking of the main road from Pendleton to Lower Irlam was introduced and toll bars were opened at Higher Irlam and Lower Irlam. The increase in costs of the Highway eventually led to the construction of the Manchester to Liverpool Railway and within twelve months of its opening, the toll bars were closed.

In the late 1700s the draining and cultivation of Chat Moss commenced, but it was not until about 1820 that farming began to have any degree of success. Later, the expectation of a railway through Chat Moss increased the acreage under cultivation. Originally there were only smallholdings, but these gradually expanded. In some cases syndicates were formed and large tracts of land were brought under cultivation.

Agriculture and weaving were the main occupations until the introduction of fustian cutting in Cadishead in 1837, and later in Irlam. Weaving gradually ceased as more families became fustian cutters. However, in the 1880s a slump in the trade occurred and many families faced starvation. Fortunately work began on the cutting of the Manchester Ship Canal and the area was gradually transformed from a rural area into an industrial one. The work brought in many strangers and their families, causing serious accommodation problems.

The opening of the Manchester Ship Canal in 1894 brought our own Industrial Revolution, with the new works opening along the whole length of the waterway. Irlam Urban District Council came into being in 1894. By 1920, the whole district had completely changed, with a great influx of workers and their families. Two great housing estates were built: the Victory Site in Cadishead and the Margarine Site in Irlam, to help ease the housing problems.

Up to the end of the nineteenth century the Manchester to Liverpool stage and mail coach called at the Nag's Head, Irlam, the Ship Hotel in Irlam - then known as Irlam Green - and the Coach and Horses in Cadishead. After the First World War Mr Robey, the landlord of the Ship Hotel, began to run a charabanc nicknamed *'The Yellow Peril'*. A Mr Cordingley opened up in opposition with a modern vehicle known as the *'Tres Bon'*. Lancashire United Transport bought out Mr Robey and commenced a regular service between Hollins Green, through the district and on to Swinton. Eventually this was joined by Salford Corporation in a Manchester to Warrington service and Selnec later took over the business.

Butcher's boys and bread vans are now a thing of the past; today we frequent supermarkets and large stores, leaving the once busy and prosperous small, local shops to be converted back to private residences once more. Since the closure of the larger works such as the Lancashire Steel Works, the CWS Soap Works, the Margarine works and Royles Engineering Works, smaller industries have sprung up needing fewer employees. The district is changing still, as it is now gradually being turned into a residential area.

Cyril Wheaton (President)
Irlam, Cadishead and District Local History Society

The River Irwell - the Old River - looking towards The Boat public house, *c.* 1891. Haymaking is being carried out in the adjoining fields and the Manchester Ship Canal is in the process of being built.

One
The Rural Scene

Harvest time on the Moss, *c.* 1910.

Aerial view of Irlam and Cadishead from west to east. The Manchester Ship Canal forms the boundary between Irlam and Partington. The main industrial sites of Lancashire Tar Distillers Ltd, Lancashire Steel Works and the two CWS works can be seen in the strip of land between the A57 road and the canal.

Lytherton Farm, which stood on the corner of Lord Street and Liverpool Road, Cadishead. The Wesleyan School can just be seen in the background.

Threshing time at Limefield Farm - now occupied by the Salvation Army 'Citadel' in Cadishead.

Barton Grange Farm on Irlam Moss, with proud occupants Mr and Mrs Henry Goodier and their baby outside the rose covered front door, *c.* 1885.

Barton Grange Farm, Irlam, *c.* 1890, showing the farmer with his beautifully dressed horse, complete with horse brasses and bells.

Celery growing on the Moss in 1908.

One of the earliest farm houses to be built on Irlam Moss was Moss Cottage, complete with water barrel and a huge, heavy chimney.

Rocket House on Irlam Moss - so named because fireworks were made here in the early 1900s.

Crossfield House Farm in 1886, which stood on the area now known as the Crossfield Estate, Higher Irlam; it was formerly occupied by the Gleave family.

Two
'The Big Ditch'

The construction of Irlam Locks in May 1893; because of soft sand in this area, over 10,000 tons of cement had to be poured in to make solid foundations.

The construction of the Ship Canal near Cadishead, *c*. 1890. Note the absence of any form of mechanical digging. Vast armies of navvies were employed using only picks and shovels in the early days.

Dutchmen were employed on certain sections of the canal on facine work: planting and weaving willows to stabilise the soil. This view was taken in April 1891, near the Irlam Ferry.

The canal workings became a small township, with mission huts and schools together with accommodation huts. This view shows a typical stall for clothing in about 1892.

Visitors came from all over the country to view the building of the canal. This group arrived in style at the Irlam Boat Hotel in June 1890.

As the Ship Canal is also the main drainage channel for various small rivers and streams, much silt and sediment enters it. The Manchester Ship Canal dredger, the *Medlock*, is shown here lifting the silt into a barge alongside. Note the early locomotive and wagons on the opposite bank.

It was most unusual to see Royal Navy ships on the Canal. This 1930s view shows HMS *Bristol* leaving Irlam Locks and proceeding under the high level railway viaduct towards Liverpool. Note the four funnels, the peculiar bridge and the guns aligned along the ship's sides.

After discharging their cargoes, ships normally had to go to the Manchester Docks to turn to go to sea. This is a successful attempt to turn a ship in the area below Irlam Locks, with the tugs *Irlam* (a paddle tug) and *Cadishead*, *c.* 1950.

Manchester was the headquarters for the fleet of cargo ships trading under the title of *Manchester Liners*. They plied the shipping route through the St Lawrence Seaway and regularly took the prize for the first ship to dock after the winter. The Manchester Ship Canal tug, *Archer*, is shown with the *Manchester Regiment* in tow, approaching Irlam Locks around 1952.

Most of the domestic waste generated in the cities of Manchester and Salford was brought down the Ship Canal by special barges. Here a grab crane at Boysnope Wharf unloads the waste into wagons of the narrow gauge railway for disposal on Chat Moss in the 1930s.

A ferry man takes passengers across the Canal at Irlam Ferry, at the end of Ferryhill Road. Note the bicycle in the old ferry boat. Vehicles were taken across the ferry on a pontoon, pulled by a winch. Originally, cattle were also transported across this way.

In 1965 the Manchester Ship Canal improved the ferry service with the introduction of the new ferry *Traverse*, which was a very revolutionary ship in so far as the propulsion was by water jet. Unfortunately this was not a success as the intakes were all too regularly blocked by rubbish and the like. This view shows the ferry about to leave the Irlam stage for the Flixton bank. Note the old ferry boat still moored at the side 'just in case'.

Bob's Lane Ferry, at Cadishead, was known at one time as 'Pollard's Ferry' and later, as 'Old Col's Ferry'.

A souvenir medal. One side, seen here, depicts the various statistical details involved in the Canal's construction. The reverse wishes success to the Ship Canal and the Thirlmere water supply.

A popular souvenir of the day to celebrate the opening of the Manchester Ship Canal.

Three
The Industrial Boom

EDGAR BARKER
(Dad)

The entire staff of the Co-operative Wholesale Society (CWS) Soap Works in 1920.

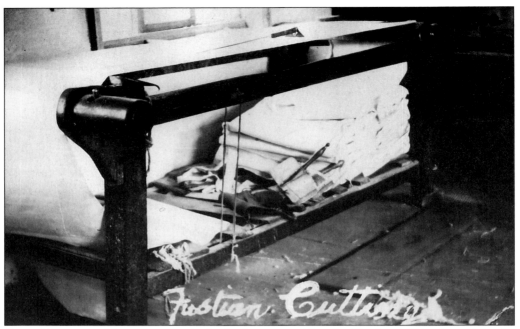

One of the types of fustian cutting beds which were used locally. The 'special' knife used for the cutting lies on top of the bed, which was about six feet in length.

This particular fustian cutting shop stood in Moss Lane, Cadishead.

Kinder McDougall & Co. came to Cadishead in 1905 and the production of wallpaper commenced in 1907. This photograph shows one of the modern printers, installed in about 1910.

Delivery of a new lorry at the Kinder McDougall works. The company ceased the production of wallpaper in 1941 as raw material was not available. Instead they produced war equipment, including parts for tanks. Paper making was in production by 1950, but transferred to Pendleton in 1952. The company still produces inks for the paper trade.

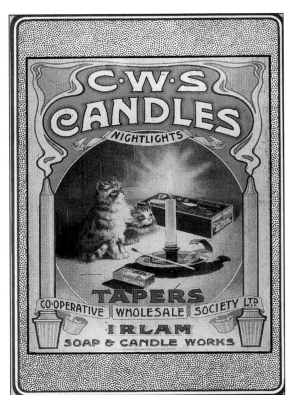

The CWS set up in Irlam around 1891, having bought a plot of land from the Manchester Ship Canal (MSC) Company. By 1909 over 700 people were employed in the manufacture of soap and allied products. This advert is from the 1920s.

Some of the men in the early days of the CWS Soap & Candle Works.

The main CWS Soap & Candle Works in 1900, showing the old railway line from Manchester to Liverpool which was disused when the Manchester Ship Canal was cut. Note that the products produced included lard.

Most raw material for the CWS Soap & Candle Works was brought in by ship via the Canal. Here a ship is unloading at the Co-op wharf in about 1910, whilst an immaculate MSC engine shunts wagons belonging to the Cheshire Lines Committee. The gable ended factory in the middle distance is still used by a Wines and Spirits company.

To keep abreast of modern soap manufacturers, the CWS had a first class laboratory, shown here, c. 1900. Note the absence of white coats, safety glasses and rubber gloves.

When the soap had been cut into bars, girls were employed to pack them into cardboard boxes and finally, into wooden crates. This view from 1901 shows the soap travelling along the conveyor belt ready to be packed.

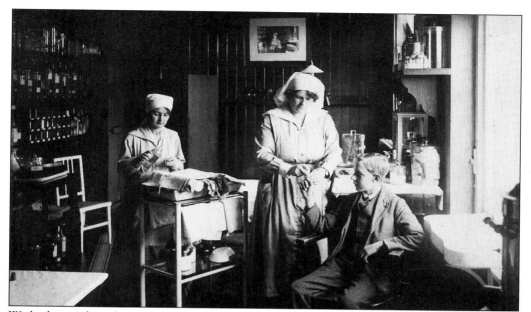

With the modern factory came services such as a first aid room, a fire fighting team and a flourishing social life. Here the head nurse, Miss Reakie, and her assistant, Miss Ashton, attend to patient Edward Thomason in 1930.

The staff of the CWS Soap Works, Irlam, in their office in 1925. In the centre is Mr Alfred Turner, after whom the Central School was renamed.

Because of the increased demand for soap after the First World War, a new factory was built in 1921/22. This view shows the main entrance and the very modern factory in the background.

The last locomotive working in the soap works was a fireless type. High pressure steam was fed into the boiler via the pipe shown at the front of the loco in this view from 1960. The driver is Mr E. Bickerton; the engine is now in Princes Park for the benefit of local children.

After the Second World War, workers had more say in the running of companies. Shown here are the members of the works' council in 1951.

The works' fire brigade after winning the inter company Challenge Shield, c. 1955.

The final day, 6 September 1959, of the soap works' rail service is shown here on the approach to Irlam main line station. In the middle distance is a Liverpool to Manchester express charging up the incline over the MSC; the first coach is in the experimental BR colours of 'blood and custard'. The cooling towers and chimneys of the Lancashire Steel Manufacturing Company are shown in the background. Today only the main line remains.

To enable their workers to get to and from the works, the company had a service linked to Irlam station. Driver Byrom is shown ready to take staff to the main line station.

In March 1932, the Duke of York, later King George VI, paid a visit to Irlam. This photograph shows him leaving the Margarine works with the girls looking on.

Inside the Margarine works in 1935 girls are packing Purple Seal products first into cartons, and then into wooden boxes. Note the hammer and box of nails for the last girl to secure the lid.

The staff of one of the departments of the Margarine works get together in their smart overalls for a group photograph, *c.* 1920s.

The Margarine works' fire brigade were very proficient throughout their existence. Here they are after one of their successful competitions in the 1930s.

The Hulme Patent Advertising Match Company commenced production in Irlam in 1895 where it produced the first non-poisonous matches in England. The company was noted for the cleanliness of its work.

Boys filling racks of book matches for drying, *c.* 1903.

35

In 1918 the match company turned to a new industry - the manufacture of non-returnable fruit 'packages'. They became the British Basket & Besto Co. Ltd and finally closed in 1965. The girls are shown packing baskets in 1936.

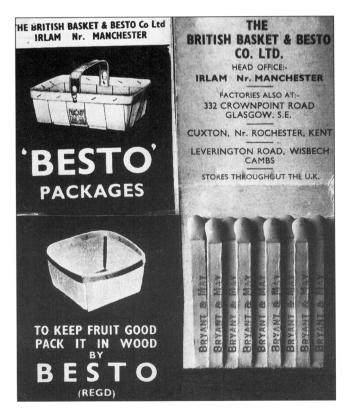

The Besto book match cover.

Lancashire Tar Distillers, now known as Lanstar Ltd, was established in 1928. Employees are shown outside the new canteen when it was opened in 1950.

Lancashire Tar Distillers, Liverpool Road, Cadishead, showing the old wooden offices and the weighbridge before 1940.

Royle's Engineering Ltd was founded in Manchester in 1874. These premises in Irlam were opened in 1900, and this photograph was taken in 1916 with the Globe Picture Palace next door. The wagon load of produce would have been on the way to the Manchester markets.

Royle's Ltd first produced articles for the domestic market, and this view shows one of their patented self-pouring teapots in action. The gentleman 'brewing-up' was James Johnson, a former President of the local history society.

In 1910 work started on the construction of the newly formed Partington Steel & Iron Company. The first contract was for a good, substantial office to be erected. This is that office in 1912.

A working committee for the company was set up in April 1911. The members were, from left to right: Mr A.H. Cooper (managing director), Mr P.S.J. Cooper (assistant manager), Mr J. Bletchlet (board member), Mr P. Rylands (board member), Mr G.R. Dobson (works secretary), Mr M. Forster (assistant secretary), Mr Lewis (chief engineer), Mr H. Loxley (chief electrical engineer), Mr L. Williams (chief draughtsman), Mr Jones (office manager), Mr Martin (blast furnace manager), Mr J.V. Morgan (steel plant manager) and Mr H. Sissons (chief chemist).

An artist's general view of the works in the early 1920s.

An early slag tip near Atherton Lane in 1915, nicknamed 'Alabama'. The slag came from the new blast furnaces and would be crushed at the plant in the background, then sold as a by-product for the road material, Tar Macadam - more familiar today as tarmac.

The 'E' steel furnace and crew in 1916, which included J. Stokes, A. Lawton, T. Kendrocks and J. Smith.

The blast furnace crushing plant, where the crushed slag was graded before being mixed with the tar for the production of Tar Macadam.

An early view of the works whilst under construction in 1913.

In 1930 the Lancashire Steel Corporation was formed, taking over the assets of the Pearson Knowles Coal & Iron Co., the Partington Steel & Iron Co. and the Wigan Coal & Iron Co. With the considerable capital involved, extensive development commenced and this view shows the opening up of No. 1 furnace in 1929.

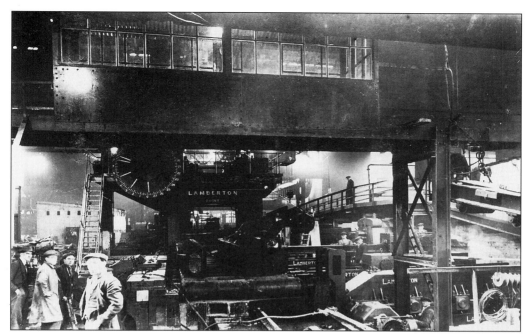

The new cogging mill at Lancashire Steel, which was commissioned in 1932.

Extensive development took place between 1930 and 1933. This included the erection of a new wharf, new coke ovens and the alteration and modernisation of the cogging mill and steel furnace. The wharf was completed in May 1932. One of the first ships to berth there was the SS *Kally* in October1932.

Workmates at the No.1 steel plant included: T. Gallagher, L. Doyle, W. Jenkinson, T. Gallagher (snr), G. Thom, W. Hood, J. Stokes, W. Wrigley and G. Roper.

MADE BY
The LANCASHIRE STEEL
CORPORATION LTD
IRLAM WORKS, M/c.
5 FEET

This three and a half ton blast furnace bell was just one of the castings made in the foundry.

Charging a steel furnace at No. 1 steel plant at the Lancashire Steel Works, Irlam.

Casting in the new foundry, c. 1956. The foundry was a very busy department where castings were made of copper, brass, steel and iron for the requirements of both the Warrington and Irlam works.

From 1953 onwards, the steam locomotives gradually became obsolete. This was one of the new diesel locomotives that replaced them.

The steel works opened an art and recreational club. Here workers are seen admiring some of their finished work; paintings, photographs, model aeroplanes and model yachts are on show. Amongst those present are Mr Murray, Tommy Gormley, Jack Colley, George Wedson and George Craven.

Four
Worship, Walks
and Wisdom

The whole of the Sunday school of St John's church in the vicarage garden in 1946.

Cadishead Wesleyan chapel, which stood at the corner of Liverpool Road and Bob's Lane. It was opened in 1874 but demolished in 1977.

Cadishead Wesley procession passing St Mary's 'Tin church' on Liverpool Road in 1920.

Irlam Wesleyan Sunday school scholars and teachers, *c.* 1914, after a Walking Day procession.

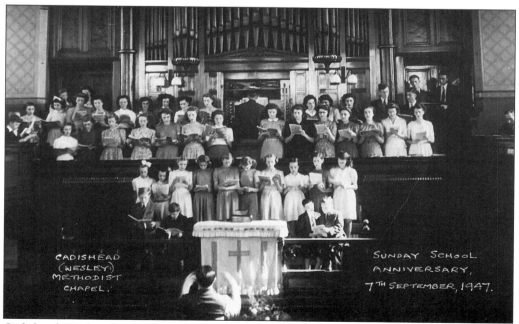

Cadishead Wesley; the Sunday school anniversary on 7 September 1947.

The pretty 'old vicarage' of St John the Baptist church, which was in a bad state of repair by 1931. It was eventually demolished and a new vicarage built in its place.

The interior of St John the Baptist church, Irlam, as it was in 1910. The font was then at the rear of the building and the old pews were still intact.

St John's church Anniversary Sunday was held on the Sunday nearest to the birth date of St John the Baptist. These young ladies were the Anniversary Girls in 1946. Vicar Lee is standing in the porch.

Members of St John's church Men's Fellowship, c. 1939, ready for a day's outing to Southport. Fourth from the left on the front row is John Gibbon MBE, who was later to be Warden Emeritus of the church.

Whit Week procession in 1927, passing Irlam Hall Lodge on Liverpool Road. It was considered an honour to carry or walk with the banner.

St John's parishioners enjoying a day trip to Alderley Edge, *c.* 1885. The gentleman circled in the photograph was Mr Henry Goodier of Barton Grange Farm, Irlam. The vicar, wearing his silk hat, is in the centre.

Today's 'Citadel' was preceded by the Salvation Army 'Hut' at the corner of Liverpool Road and New Moss Road, Cadishead. The 'Hut' was later removed to Hollins Green to be used as a scout hut.

The United Methodist church on the corner of Fairhills Road and Liverpool Road, where today's Youth Club stands. Built just after the First World War ended, it was originally part of the Oxford Road, Manchester, circuit.

St Mary's church Walking Day, passing Moss Lane, Cadishead, in about 1890.

From the 'Tin church', St Mary's acquired land in Penry Avenue, Cadishead, and parishioners 'bought' foundation stones to start the building of a new church. Some of those stones are seen here being laid.

54

Parishioners of St Mary's church enjoying a harvest supper in 1954.

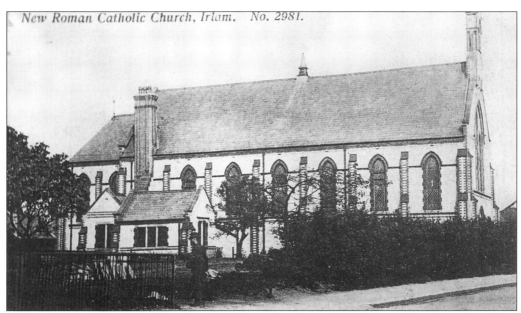

An early view of the new St Teresa's RC church on the corner of Astley Road and Liverpool Road, Irlam. The church was built in 1903 in place of the previous small chapel, and dedicated to St Teresa and in memory of Miss Belinda de Trafford, the church's benefactor.

St Teresa's Walking Day, May 1925. The procession is seen leaving Astley Road on to Liverpool Road.

St Teresa's special Walking Day passing The Arcade shops on Liverpool Road in the 1930s.

The Salvation Army Band leading a church's Walking Day with Mrs Winrow carrying the banner, *c.* 1950s.

Cadishead Congregational church on the corner of Dean Road, before the new porch was built. The building on the right was formerly the old police station. It now houses the archives for the city of Salford.

The first school to be built in the district was the Cadishead Wesleyan School in Lord Street, Cadishead, in 1807. The railings, gate and lamp post have long since gone.

These schoolboys are standing outside the Wesleyan School on the corner of Chapel Road and Liverpool Road, Irlam, c. 1905. The school was built in 1878 and closed in 1914. It is now used as a doctor's surgery.

Irlam Wesleyan School with Miss Garner and Miss Davidson in 1899.

Irlam Endowed School was endowed by John Greaves of Irlam Hall, and used as a school and chapel until St John's church was ready in 1866.

Miss Bentley, headmistress of the Endowed School, with her pupils in 1920.

The newly opened Irlam Junior Council School in 1915.

Mr Hilton, Headmaster of Irlam Junior Council School, with pupils, staff and parents at his retirement presentation.

Cadishead Junior Council School, Lord Street, which opened in 1909.

Pupils of Cadishead Council School in 1941, playing percussion instruments in a music lesson in the school hall. The conductor was Alma Westall.

Pupils of Cadishead Junior Council School in the 1930s.

Pupils of St Mary's Day School in 1918.

St Mary's Day School in John Street, Cadishead, near to Cadishead Post Office. When the new school was built in Buckingham Road, this building became a business unit.

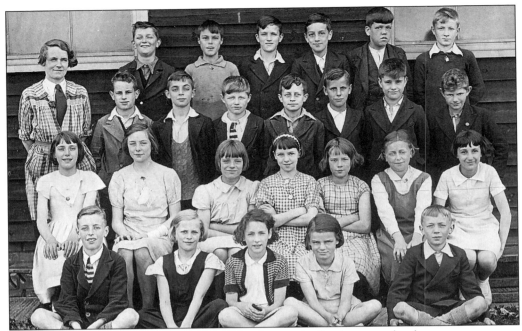

Pupils of Irlam Central School in 1927/8, the first intake for the new school.

Cadishead Senior School, Allotment Road, in 1973, which was later renamed Alfred Turner School. It is now Cadishead Junior School.

Five
The King's Highway

The Irlam toll bar was situated on the turnpike road near to what we now know as Marlborough Road. Tolls paid in 1826 were: for every cart or other carriage with two wheels, 2d, and every description of other carriages, 1d for each wheel. The tolls were finally abolished on 1 January 1892.

Goodier's bakery and shop at the junction of Boat Lane and Liverpool Road.

Higher Irlam in 1905, showing the junction of Silver Street and Liverpool Road, with the Nag's Head on the right.

This shop was in Hurst Fold, Irlam, adjoining a row of cottages, *c.* 1890s. It is now Higher Irlam Post Office.

The bus belonging to Irlam Motor Garages, parked in front of the Palace cinema (later the Savoy), *c.* 1920.

Prescott View, known locally as 'Twenty Row', Liverpool Road, Irlam, when the houses were converted into shops.

Hindley ladies' outfitters shop in The Arcade row of shops at the top of Irlam Brow in the 1930s.

Wetherall & Co. Ltd, grocers. This shop was opposite St Teresas's church on Liverpool Road, Irlam.

Openshaw House, at the corner of Prospect Road, was built by Mr Wright in 1885 and later sold to the Union Bank. In December 1950, after being empty for ten years, it was altered to house the first county branch library in the district.

Inside Seymour Mead's grocers on the main road between Albert Street and Dean Road, in 1925. You can almost smell the bacon and cheese! The chairs would have been very welcome.

Mr J.R. Tynan, the manager, on the left, and Mr W. Watkin, his assistant, stand outside Nuttall Street Co-op Stores, Cadishead. In the window is their prize winning soap display in 1938.

Melia's grocery shop near Albert Street, Cadishead, with the slogan 'The foods that make hens lay and pay'.

The hut on the left was a Working Men's Club and would later belong to the Salvation Army. On the right is the George Hotel.

Moss Lane, Cadishead, was originally one of the roads that led to the Moss. After the Manchester Ship Canal was constructed, the railway embankment cutting considerably altered the road. The band room is on the left and Barber Owen's shop, in the right corner, became affectionately known as 'Owen's College'.

An early advertisement for the Lombardian Stores which was very well known and sold all kinds of clothes, furniture, floor coverings and household items. During the 1920s it was better known for the pawn shop at the rear of the building.

The Lombardian Stores, Cadishead. In the doorway stands J.T. Booth and his sons William and John, in 1953. The previous owner was Tom Scofield who ran the shop as a pawn shop and hardware store. The Booths kept it for hardware until the early 1970s, but it was then changed to a carpet and furniture store until it closed in 1986.

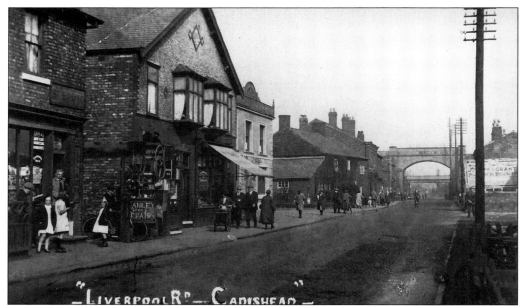

Liverpool Road, Cadishead, showing both the railway bridges. The Railway Hotel is in the centre.

A view of Heyes Road, Cadishead, from Liverpool Road. Peter Barrow's wooden 'shop' is evident in the left corner.

LIVERPOOL. ROAD. CADISHEAD, TO. WARRINGTON.

Liverpool Road, Cadishead, opposite to where the Derby cycle store now stands, on what was to be the site of the Lombardian Stores. Note the end of a fustian cutting shop, part of which still remains.

LIVERPOOL-ROAD CADISHEAD   JULY-1916   RE.

This view from 1916 shows the Jubilee Lamp on the right of the road and the Coach and Horses on the left.

Cadishead railway station as it was before the Manchester Ship Canal was constructed. The station was later built on a different level to accommodate the rise over the Canal.

The completed Irlam station, with the station master's house on the left. The ladies' waiting room on the right always had a fire burning during the winter.

A Co-op ladies' outing leaving by charabanc from outside the Cadishead Co-op shop near the Lion Hotel, Cadishead, 1912.

The 'Wedding Car' belonging to the firm of Bert Johnson, complete with liveried chauffeur.

Irlam UDC workmen and their lorry, working on one of the new council estates in the district, *c.* 1920.

Maypole Dairy steam driven vehicle outside the old council offices, Irlam, on its way to deliver goods to the dairy in Cadishead.

A cold, snowy scene in 1905 showing the Old Nags Head in Irlam, with its advert for 'Good Stabling'.

An early photograph of the Ship Hotel in Irlam, before it was plastered and colour washed.

Angling matches have been held on the River Irwell - the Old River - for many years. Here we see the fishermen being instructed in 1900 before a competition. Incidentally, it is just 100 years ago that the County Palatine Angler's Association restocked the river, possibly for the Jubilee celebrations.

Cadishead and District 'Flying Club' - for pigeon fanciers - in 1929 outside the Railway Hotel, now the Plough. They are all ready for an outing in a canvas topped charabanc.

Six

'Curtain Up'

Mr Hayden Ellwood, proprietor of the Globe cinema, *c.* 1920. Mr Ellwood produced 'live' shows as well as 'talking pictures'.

Cadishead Belles from Cadishead Wesley church in 1918, looking very demure.

LANCASHIRE TAR DISTILLERS LTD.

JOB CARD

COST: 11s. 6d.   JOB: DANCE   DATE: 20th DEC. 1968

DETAILS OF WORK TO BE CARRIED OUT.

LOCATION: CADISHEAD CONSERVATIVE CLUB

STARTING TIME: 8.0 P.M.

COMPLETION TIME: 1.0 A.M.

BONUS: BUFFET AND SPOT PRIZES

JOB INSTRUCTION: ENJOY YOURSELF

Programme of Dances

Irlam Council Sc

STAFF
DANCE

Friday, Feb.16

M.C. - Mr. H. HILT

Stewards:
Mr. Blackwell, Mr. Derby
Mr. Parsons, Mrs. Hulme
Jack, Miss Rhys, Miss B
Miss Thompson, Miss An
Miss Higginson.

Whist at 7-15 Pro

Tickets, 4s. 6d. e
And are NOT Transf

An unusual ticket for a dance given by Lancashire Tar Distillers in 1968. No doubt the ticket was thought up by someone in the drawing office or the fitting shop. In contrast, this is a dance programme from the 1930s for a staff dance and whist drive in Irlam Council School, complete with cord to hang on a lady's wrist.

A bazaar, held in the old British Legion building, obviously being opened by local dignitaries, *c.* 1920.

A happy gathering of members and friends of the Royal British Legion awaiting their meal in 1950.

Irlam Spinsters Band outside the old Irlam Vicarage, *c.* 1890.

Greasy log sports in the park, c. 1920s.

Cadishead Operatic Prize Band in the early 1900s, were a 'comedy' band which provided local entertainment. All the instruments were deliberately faulty.

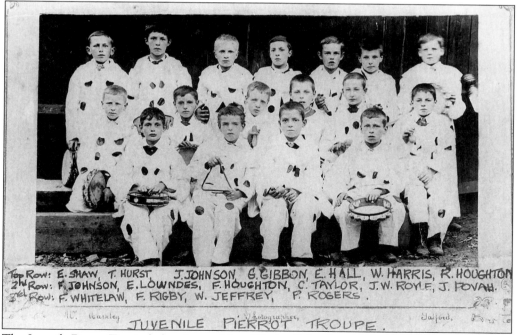

Top Row: E. SHAW, T. HURST, J. JOHNSON, G. GIBBON, E. HALL, W. HARRIS, R. HOUGHTON
2nd Row: F. JOHNSON, E. LOWNDES, F. HOUGHTON, C. TAYLOR, J. W. ROYLE, J. POVAH.
3rd Row: F. WHITELAW, F. RIGBY, W. JEFFREY, P. ROGERS.

JUVENILE PIERROT TROUPE.

The *Juvenile Pierrot Troupe* belonging to Irlam Wesley School in 1899. The headmistress at the time was Miss Davidson, whilst Miss Higginson played the piano.

The Howmari Choir. This choir originated from the Mary Wright Girls' Choir and was formed in about 1948. The original conductor was Oliver Howarth.

The Irlcadians. The Irlam Male Voice Choir, first formed in December 1945, was originally called the Irlam and Cadishead Male Voice Choir, the first conductor being Mr C. Hargreaves, the Headmaster of Irlam Council School. In 1947 the name was changed to the Irlcadians. From 1965 the conductor was Oliver Howarth but the singers are now known as the Irlam Male Voice Choir.

Irlam and Cadishead Choral Society performing *The Emerald Isle* on 5 April 1933 in Irlam Conservative Club.

Ladies of the Cadishead Wesleyan church holding a fancy dress party in 1915, possibly as a war effort. Note the fortune teller and the suffragette.

St Teresa's also had a dramatic society and the plays were performed in St Teresa's School at the top of Clarendon Road, Irlam. In about 1948, the musical play, *The Arcadians*, by Lionel Monckton was produced.

St Paul's Amateur Dramatic Society was formed in 1930. Performances took place in St Paul's schoolroom, Liverpool Road, Irlam, (now a doctor's surgery). They produced about three plays a year. *The Unguarded Hour*, seen above, was produced in 1950.

Cadishead Congregational church was the venue for a musical operetta for the children called *The Butterfly Queen*. Performances were held in the church until the Sunday school was built in the 1930s.

Irlam and Cadishead Youth Club provided a variety of activities under the leadership of Wilf James, assisted by Mrs Carine. Meetings were held in Cadishead Senior School, Allotment Road, Cadishead. The Youth Club Players produced *The Happiest Days of Your Life* in February 1952.

There are records of Irlam Brass Band going back to the 1880s. In 1882 they were assisting the Blue Ribbon Army by leading their procession through the district to display their new silk banner. In 1886 they staged a brass band concert on a field near Irlam railway station and bands came from far and near to take part. Throughout the years the band has fulfilled many successful engagements. Rehearsals are now held in their own band room near Princes Park. The band is led by Stan Crawford. The first bandsman on the left is Ron Hesford.

Cadishead Band was formed between 1875 and 1878, and it is recorded that they were accepting regular engagements at local events in the 1880s. After a variety of rehearsal venues, the band now meets at the old fire station in Clarendon Road, Irlam. The photograph is from 1958/9. The leader is Frank Tattersall who was a well known preacher.

Seven

Play the Game

St Mary's hockey team. Sport played a major part in local activities after the First World War. As well as hockey these included football, cricket, tennis, bowls and netball. The gentleman in the centre of the picture, Mr Leach, was a prominent member of the church and no doubt allowed matches to be played on his field.

During the First World War many events took place to raise funds for parcels and supplies for the local people away on active service. This particular football match between two teams of ladies from the soap works was played on the sports ground of the steel works in Cooper Road. Admission was 4d.

Cadishead Wesley ladies' cricket team, *c.* 1922. The ground used was opposite the chapel on the main road, access being from the school in Lord Street.

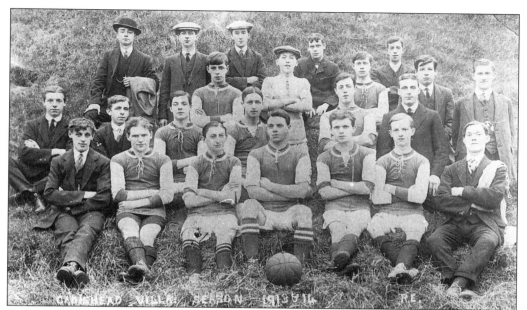

Cadishead Villa football team, 1913/14. Most likely many of the team later 'did their bit' in the First World War.

The Steel Works Club had several teams taking part in various sports. The photograph shows their football team in about 1920.

Early this century there were many local cricket teams. Here we have the champions from 1906 until 1908.

Cadishead Wesley Cricket Club, *c.* 1923, outside their pavilion. Revd Walter Hudson, the minister, favoured the match by his presence.

St John's Tennis Club members outside their club house in Irlam around 1918. This is now a private house, namely Cadby Lodge.

Irlam Central School netball team, *c.* 1948.

The CWS Soap Works team in 1934. Members included, from left to right: R. Minshull, J. Yates, J. Lythgoe, W. McGuire, G. Wenham, R. James, T. Hampson, J. Hutson, R. Hill, J. Owen, J. Taylor, A. Perrin, G. Byrom, C. Threadgold, R. Drum, J. Scallon, C. Ashton and H. Dixon.

Office members of the Lancashire Steel Works, Irlam, and their opponents from the Warrington office pause during a hockey match in 1933.

Irlam and Cadishead Youth Club, under the auspices of Lancashire Education Committee, met regularly at Cadishead Senior School in Allotment Road, for all types of sporting activities. One of their two netball teams is seen here.

Here we have the archery group with the chief warden, Wilf James.

Unsworth's Social bowling green and billiard hall, opened in 1909, was well known for its bowlers for it was here that many of the local men trundled their first 'wood'. Being a teetotal club it was well patronised by the local youths.

Bowlers at the new Liberal Club in 1910. The building later became the premises for the Cadishead Conservative Association.

Eight
People and Places

May Queen celebrations in Moss Lane, Cadishead, *c.* 1903, complete with a maypole and delightfully dressed children.

Irlam May Festival, 1908. It was the fashion to carry a shepherd's crook, decorated with flowers, instead of a bouquet.

A happy, expectant crowd amidst the bunting, await the arrival of King Edward VII on Irlam Brow in 1909.

A large crowd of excited children await the matinee opening of the new Palace cinema at the top of Irlam Brow. It was later called the Savoy, but was demolished to make way for a car park.

A picnic outing to Lower Peover for the regulars of the Ship Hotel, Irlam, in July 1909.

Mr George Thomas, of Irlam Hall, opening the new recreation ground for Irlam Urban District Council in 1912. The recreation ground was established on part of the Irlam Hall Estate.

The grand opening of the first Irlam Social Club in Cutnook Lane, Irlam. Mr Standish, first on the left of the front row, was one of the instigators of the club who bought the old army hut for £700.

Little sailor boys get restless whilst waiting for the King on Irlam Brow in 1909.

Cadishead Brownies in 1932. A smart and cheerful group wear the older type of uniform. Guide and Brownie leaders always wore enormous gauntlet gloves as part of their uniform.

Irlam and District Boy Scouts, wearing original scout hats, *c.* 1920.

VIPs and staff of Irlam UDC await the arrival of the Prince of Wales in 1921 outside the old council offices, now demolished, which used to stand at the corner of Clarendon Road and Liverpool Road.

Mr Motley, the coal merchant of Hayes Road, Cadishead, loaned his coal cart for the May Queen in Cadishead, *c.* 1900.

The Poplars, No. 168 Liverpool Road, Cadishead. Built in 1792, the shell of the building is still inside the present garage.

Members of St Mary's Ladies' Sewing Guild with Mrs Yeadon in the centre of the back row, who was Headmistress of the Day School.

After hostilities ceased at the end of the Second World War, the vast influx of demobbed servicemen had an urgent need of houses. One stop-gap idea was prefabricated housing, as seen here. This is the only prefabricated house still standing in its original condition in Fairhills Road.

Left: Ivy Cottage, originally one of the lodges of Irlam Hall, opposite Chapel Road. Right: Mr W. Fairhurst, blacksmith of Moss Lane, Cadishead, with his family, *c.* 1890.

Left: Miss Amelia Gell, district nurse and midwife, 1911. Right: Edmund Potts and staff outside his thriving grocery in Allotment Road.

Mrs Nancy Lee, the wife of Vicar Lee of St John's church, Irlam, officially launching the Sea Scouts' boat named the *Nancy Lee* in her honour. The launching took place at the Fairhills Road end of the Old River in about 1930.

Birthday party in 1928. The birthday girl, Margaret Tynan (now Margaret Bancroft) was 7 years old at the time.

Mr John Gibbon MBE, Warden Emeritus and life long worshipper at Irlam church, points to the carving of an angel on the unfinished table which was made by Vicar Lee just before his death in 1958. The table is still standing in the church today. Mr Gibbon was President of the Local History Society prior to his death.

Mr James Goodier of Hulmes Farm, Irlam, who was a well known local historian and the first President of Irlam, Cadishead and District Local History Society.

May Day carnival in Cadishead in about 1920. The float is passing the Irlam and Cadishead Motor Company's Garage, which later became Morgan's Garage.

Barton was the first municipal airport in Britain and the original hangar is shown here. Manchester's coat of arms is still inscribed on the gable end. The aerodrome is still used for light aircraft and helicopters and now also houses a museum.

Members of St John's church on a day trip to the seaside in about 1925, all looking very smart in their spats, feather boas and Sunday hats.

Mr George Whitfield, on the far left, and his family outside their cottage around 1880. The cottage was on the left of the Derby shop near to Cadishead Bridge.

Irlam and Cadishead have a vigorous and flourishing Probus Club. In 1980 Mr Cyril Wheaton, a noted local historian with many booklets to his credit, accepted the position of President from Mr Les Hall. Mr Wheaton is at present the President of Irlam, Cadishead and District Local History Society.

The full staff of Irlam Urban District Council at the end of March 1974, prior to the reorganisation of local government.

Nine

The Halls

Irlam Hall was built over 500 years ago and was inhabited by many different families over the centuries. These included the Hultons, the Lathoms and the Greaves. However the last owner, Mr George Thomas, seen above, is the best remembered, especially for his benevolence to the local community. He gave land to the local council for the establishment of a recreation ground and later, Princes Park was provided to commemorate the visit of the Prince of Wales in 1921. In his will in 1927 he left the hall, grounds and other lands to the Irlam Urban District Council. The hall was used for all types of meetings until it was considered unsafe in the late 1940s. It was finally demolished in 1952.

George Thomas as depicted on a Christmas card in 1915.

An interior view of one of the rooms taken early this century. Note the ornate fireplace and the oil lamp.

Lodge   Irlam Hall gates.

Irlam Hall lodge and gates at the main entrance were taken down in order to widen the main road, the A57, which ran through the district.

When the hall was finally demolished, there were some features well worth preserving. These included the especially fine carved front door.

115

Longfield Lodge, Cadishead, was originally a small, private school owned by Mr Garlick and known locally as Garlick's Academy. It became so successful that extensions had to be built to accommodate all the pupils and staff. After his death, the property was eventually sold and became a private residence. In later years the lodge was sold to the local authority, who, after alterations, used it as a local clinic for the whole district. A mortuary was added at a later date but the building is now a private residence.

Hayes Hall, Cadishead. The old hall went back many years and was built in three distinct sections. The first section was made of wattle and daub which was partly built over by the second phase. A date stone on the gable end read '1671 AD'. The final phase was completed in the nineteenth century. The early inhabitants were named Heyes or Hayes, and they lived there until the 1880s. It was later owned by a Mr Fell and then by Henry Leach, and the Manchester Ship Canal Company bought some of the land in 1888. The hall was finally demolished in 1960.

Ten

'Lest We Forget'

These gallant men, of all ages, answered the call of duty to join Kitchener's Army on 9 November 1914.

These young ladies were 'knitters' for the war-wounded troops. To thank them, the army 'kit' was loaned to them for this photograph by visiting soldiers in 1918.

A group of Irlam and Cadishead Red Cross workers outside Irlam Hall, c. 1916. Mr George Thomas, the owner, is on the far left.

War Memorial, Princes Park, Irlam.

This First World War Memorial was erected in about 1920 in what is now known as Princes Park. It was later demolished and a cenotaph was erected in its place to commemorate the dead of two World Wars.

The ARP control centre was situated at the rear of the old council office in Clarendon Road. This view shows volunteers testing this 'nerve' centre at its opening in March 1940. From left to right: Mr Jones (controller), Mr H. Nurse (technical officer), Mr S. Bowman (surveyors officer), Mr F. Exley (communications officer), Mr D. Neville and Miss M. Morriss (chart writers). Mr Nurse is plotting on the large map at the rear of the building.

Wings for Victory, 1943. Irlam and Cadishead people have always been generous, as can be seen from the results shown on the board.

The British Restaurant on Liverpool Road, Irlam, was open to the public from Monday 17 January 1944, for 'cash and carry' from 11.20 am-12 noon and as a restaurant from 12 noon to 2.00 pm. The photograph shows staff from the restaurant taking a break between serving 1s 9d meals. Royle's Engineering Works can be seen nearby.

ECCLES & DISTRICT CO-OPERATIVE SOCIETY LIMITED.
Education   **Committee.**

In aid of the Red Cross Society, St. John Ambulance Association
and the Co-operative Employees' Active Service Fund.

IN THE CO-OPERATIVE HALL, SILVER ST., HIGHER IRLAM,

ON SUNDAY, JULY 21st. 1940. at 8 p.m.

GRAND CONCERT

BY THE IRLAM & CADISHEAD ORCHESTRAL SOCIETY

(Assisted by Mr. George Morrall Elocutionist).

Conductor : Mr. Harold Fairhurst.

Principal Violin & Leader Mr. Harold Hughes.

Chairman Mr. E. Channon (Education Committee)

Admission by Programme 1/- (Children under 16 half price).

The whole of the proceeds will be given to the Funds stated above.

The concert ticket is self explanatory but is typical of the type of fund raising event carried out throughout the district to aid the War Effort.

The steel works section of the Home Guard Decontamination Squad on exercise.

Camouflaged centres at the steel works. Note the Morris and Ford cars with edgings so that they could be seen in the blackout.

Members of the local Civil Defence Corps and the WVS pose for a photograph, *c.* 1943-44.

Irlam Home Guards on a march through Irlam, *c.* 1943, and as usual the local children accompany them.

Ladies of the WVS form part of a civic parade, passing the old Council Offices, during the Second World War.

A Home Guard event in the grounds of the Alfred Turner School in 1940.

The dispersal of local services at the end of the Second World War in 1945 on the Alfred Turner school field.

Victory celebrations for children in Irlam Junior school in 1945, complete with a cake.

Acknowledgements

The author is grateful to the following friends for without their help, this book would have been impossible: Ann Arnold, Donald Palmer, Cyril Wheaton, Frances Pilling and James Ashton for his photography.

Thanks must also go to the following organisations who have given permission to reproduce certain photographs: *The Advertiser*, Aerial Views Ltd, Manchester Records Office, Surveyor's Dept, Manchester, *Warrington Guardian* and Salford Education and Leisure Directorate.

Finally, thanks must go to friends and members of the Irlam, Cadishead and District Local History Society who have kindly loaned their photographs.

A Cadishead view card which actually includes Warburton Bridge, Princes Park in Irlam, Bob's Lane Ferry and two views of Liverpool Road.

Index